HAWKS

BIRDS OF PREY

BY NATHAN SOMMER

EPIC

BELLWETHER MEDIA • MINNEAPOLIS, MN

EPIC BOOKS are no ordinary books. They burst with intense action, high-speed heroics, and shadows of the unknown. Are you ready for an Epic adventure?

This edition first published in 2019 by Bellwether Media, Inc.

No part of this publication may be reproduced in whole or in part without written permission of the publisher. For information regarding permission, write to Bellwether Media, Inc., Attention: Permissions Department, 6012 Blue Circle Dr. Minnetonka, MN 55343.

Library of Congress Cataloging-in-Publication Data

Names: Sommer, Nathan, author.
Title: Hawks / by Nathan Sommer.
Description: Minneapolis, MN : Bellwether Media, Inc., 2019. | Series: Epic.
  Birds of Prey | Audience: Age 7-12. | Audience: Grade 2 to 7. | Includes
  bibliographical references and index.
Identifiers: LCCN 2018003576 (print) | LCCN 2018006814 (ebook) | ISBN
  9781626178809 (hardcover : alk. paper)| ISBN 9781681036267 (ebook)
Subjects: LCSH: Hawks–Juvenile literature. | Birds of prey–Juvenile
  literature.
Classification: LCC QL696.F32 (ebook) | LCC QL696.F32 S664 2019 (print) | DDC
  598.9/44–dc23
LC record available at https://lccn.loc.gov/2018003576

TABLE OF CONTENTS

HOT PURSUIT

The speedy northern goshawk blasts through the treetops. This hungry **predator** hopes to make a catch.

The hawk flies quickly after a pheasant below. The chase is on!

5

The goshawk zips around trees easily. It catches up to the pheasant in no time. The hawk captures the **prey** with its feet. Then it lands on the ground to feast!

WHAT ARE HAWKS?

RED-TAILED HAWK

Hawks are small- to medium-sized birds of prey. They live on every **continent** except Antarctica.

Hawks are some of the most skilled fliers in the world. They are known for their speed. The fastest hawks can fly more than 120 miles (193 kilometers) per hour!

TINY HAWK

Fun Size Predators

Hawks are strong, but they can also be tiny. The smallest are shorter than a box of cereal!

GRAY HAWK

Some hawks live in open areas where they can see everything. They usually have long wings to soar through the air.

Other hawks prefer forests. They often have short wings and long tails. These help them fly quickly through the trees!

TYPES OF HAWKS

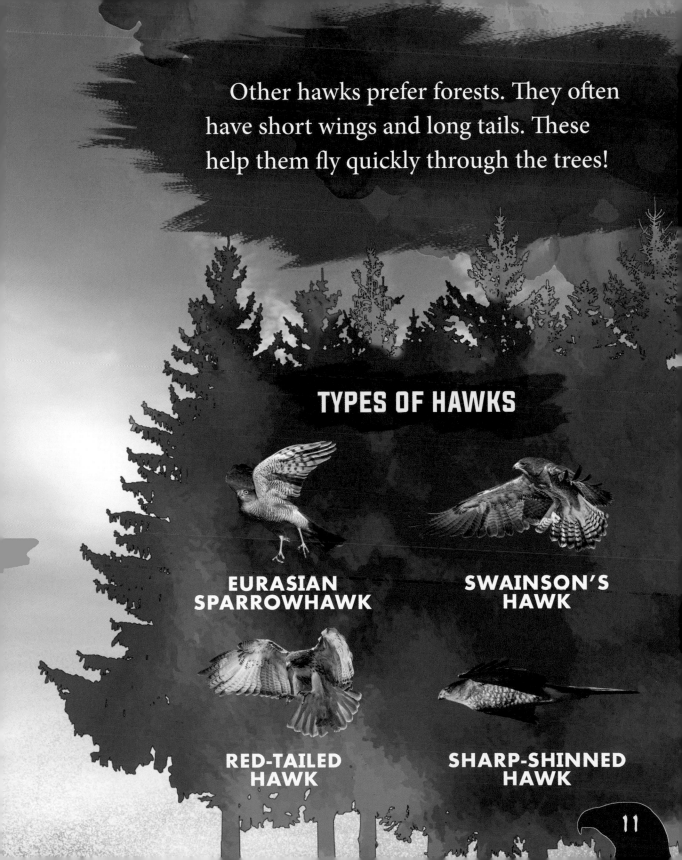

EURASIAN SPARROWHAWK

SWAINSON'S HAWK

RED-TAILED HAWK

SHARP-SHINNED HAWK

BIRD HUNTERS

Hawks are **carnivores**. Small birds are one of hawks' favorite foods. They also eat **reptiles** and **rodents**.

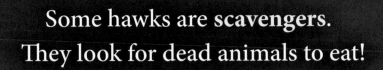

Some hawks are **scavengers**.
They look for dead animals to eat!

COMMON BUZZARD

Picky Eaters

Some hawks do not like the taste of feathers. When they catch a bird, they pluck off every single feather before eating their meal!

COOPER'S HAWK

Backyard Bullies
Some hawks hunt for prey at bird feeders. This makes them an enemy to many bird lovers!

Hawks mostly hunt during the day. They dart between trees to find their next meal. Others **perch** on tall trees or poles to watch for prey.

Many hawks are **pursuit** hunters. They hide until prey is near. Then they pop out to surprise and chase their meals.

EURASIAN
SPARROWHAWK

In open areas, many hawks fly low. Some even run on the ground to chase their food!

Other hawks fly up high to get a good view of prey. All hawks use their feet to catch their food.

HARRIS'S HAWK

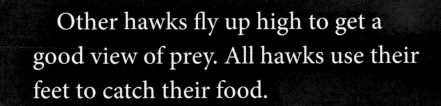

Bird Brains

Hawks are among the world's smartest birds. Many plan out their hunts and work in teams to catch prey!

Strong, curved **talons** keep prey from escaping. Hooked beaks allow hawks to eat quickly.

18

These smart birds **adapt** to **habitats** around the world. Their speedy, skilled flying makes them successful hunters anywhere!

SHARP-SHINNED HAWK PROFILE

RED LIST STATUS: LEAST CONCERN

LEAST CONCERN	NEAR THREATENED	VULNERABLE	ENDANGERED	CRITICALLY ENDANGERED	EXTINCT IN THE WILD	EXTINCT

AVERAGE LIFE SPAN: ABOUT 3 YEARS

GREATEST HUNTING TOOL: LONG TAIL FOR CHANGING DIRECTION QUICKLY

WINGSPAN: OVER 2 FEET (0.6 METERS)

TOP SPEED: 28 MILES (45 KILOMETERS) PER HOUR; UP TO 60 MILES (96 KILOMETERS) PER HOUR DIVING

SHARP-SHINNED HAWK RANGE MAP

SHARP-SHINNED HAWK RANGE =

PREY

WARBLERS	SPARROWS	GRASSHOPPERS	MICE

GLOSSARY

adapt—to change over time to more easily survive

carnivores—animals that only eat meat

continent—a very large mass of land; there are seven continents in the world.

habitats—the homes or areas where animals prefer to live

perch—to sit in a tall spot, such as a branch or rooftop

predator—an animal that hunts other animals for food

prey—an animal that is hunted by another animal for food

pursuit—the act of chasing or following quickly

reptiles—cold-blooded animals that have backbones and lay eggs

rodents—small mammals that gnaw on their food; mice, squirrels, and beavers are all rodents.

scavengers—animals that mostly eat food that is already dead

talons—the strong, sharp claws of hawks and other birds of prey

TO LEARN MORE

At the Library

Borgert-Spaniol, Megan. *Red-Tailed Hawks*. Minneapolis, Minn.: Bellwether Media, 2015.

Hoena, Blake. *Everything Birds of Prey*. Washington, D.C.: National Geographic Kids, 2015.

Riggs, Kate. *Hawks*. Mankato, Minn.: Creative Education, 2015.

On the Web

Learning more about hawks is as easy as 1, 2, 3.

1. Go to www.factsurfer.com.

2. Enter "hawks" into the search box.

3. Click the "Surf" button and you will see a list of related web sites.

With factsurfer.com, finding more information is just a click away.

INDEX

The images in this book are reproduced through the courtesy of: Ian Duffield, cover, p. 11 (bottom left); Stephen Mcsweeny, p. 2; Vladimir Hodac, pp. 4, 5 (hawk), 6-7; Jordan Confino, p. 8; FLPA/ Alamy, p. 9; Bshumaker 17, p. 10; Erni, p. 11 (top left); txking, p. 11 (top right); rck_953 (bottom right); Neil_Burton, p. 12; Duncan Usher, p. 13; BirdImages, p. 14; Pal Hermansen/ Getty Images, p. 15; imageBROKER, p. 16; Karel Bartik, p. 17; Lisa Louise Greenhorn, p. 18; Paul S. Wolf, p. 19; Nick Saunders, p. 20; Bonnie Taylor Barry, p. 21 (left); Sharon Day, p. 21 (left middle); Rudmer Zwerver, p. 21 (right middle); Peter Eggermann, p. 21 (right).